## A NOTE FROM THE PUBLISHER

While Americans and Canadians might call the sport in this book *soccer* and its playing surface a *field*, this book—like most other English-speaking fans—uses the terms *football* and *pitch*. In Thai, the sport is called ฟุตบอล (*fut-bawn*; pronounced almost like *football*).

To my teammates, the Cafe Invaders.

— D. K.

For Quentin, Declan, Brandon, and Lindsay.

— D. P.

Text © 2023 Darshana Khiani • Illustrations © 2023 Dow Phumiruk

Published in 2023 by Eerdmans Books for Young Readers,
an imprint of Wm. B. Eerdmans Publishing Co., Grand Rapids, Michigan

www.eerdmans.com/youngreaders

32  31  30  29  28  27  26  25  24  23          1  2  3  4  5  6  7  8  9

ISBN  978-0-8028-5547-3 • Illustrations created digitally.

A catalog record of this book is available from the Library of Congress.

### Selected Sources

VICE Sports. "Thailand's Football-Crazed Fishermen and the Floating Pitch."
YouTube Video. July 8, 2014. https://www.youtube.com/watch?v=T_xTYZbQ4n4.

Nuntasinrapachai, Sompetch, and Alice Grant."TMB Panyee FC Short Film."
TMB Bank Public Company Limited, Thailand. YouTube Video. March 13, 2011.
https://www.youtube.com/watch?v=jU4oA3kkAWU.

Bohwongprasert, Yvonne. "A Local Hero Reflects on Establishing a Champion
Footsol Club in the South." *Bangkok Post*, March 25, 2011.

# BUILDING A DREAM

## How the Boys of Koh Panyee Became Champions

DARSHANA KHIANI

DOW PHUMIRUK

EERDMANS BOOKS FOR YOUNG READERS

GRAND RAPIDS, MICHIGAN

In the billowy bay waters, hidden in the shadows of towering limestone cliffs, atop a network of stilts, floats the village of Koh Panyee. In that village, a group of boys . . .

dribbled on the way to school,

kneed balls while waiting in line,

and shot goals during evening chores.

Every Saturday afternoon,
they raced along the waterfront,
through the marketplace . . .

across the rickety-crickety
walkways . . .

. . . up to Uncle Hemmin's ramshackle café.

They scrambled up front to watch . . . FOOTBALL!

*Headbutt . . . cross pass . . . bicycle kick . . . GOAL!*

"We should form a team," said Surin while bouncing a football. "Then we can compete with the mainland boys."

"Impossible," said Krit, slumping against the wooden pillar. "We don't have a pitch."

Without a pitch, how could they perfect their skills? They hung their heads in defeat—except for Surin.

"We'll practice without one," he said. "We're going to be a team!"

Lek and the younger boys cheered.

"That's ridiculous,"
said Uncle Hemmin.

"Look around."

There was no place to play . . .
anywhere.

This didn't stop the boys
from trying.

Lek juggled balls in the alleyway.

Krit dribbled down the main walkway.

Surin kicked near the pier.

They had no place to play.

"You can't play like the mainland boys. No pitch," said
Uncle Hemmin. "Stick to boat racing. It's tradition."

"This is hopeless. We'll never get good enough to compete," said a younger boy. Like players after losing a shoot-out, they trudged home.

"You really want to be football players?" said a young fisherman unloading his catch.

"I know a secret place, but it only exists during low tide."

Every afternoon, the boys' footprints littered the newly smoothed sand.

Surin chipped in the salty, sticky air.

Lek blocked in the warm sideways rain.

Krit passed in the cool, fresh breeze.

"Nothing can stop us now," said Surin
as he charged down the pitch. "We're
going to be champions!"

*Pass . . .*

*Kick . . .*

*SCORE!*

But after the next monsoon season, their dreams washed away. The village needed the beach for new homes. Men hauled stilts, hammered planks, and built homes.

Once again, the boys had no place to play.

They stopped dribbling to school and kicking during chores.

"We can't play in the alleys, the walkways, or the beach," said Krit. "We'll never be champions."

They plopped onto the steps, their heads hung in defeat—except for Lek's.

"Our people built this village over water," said Lek. "What if we made our own place to play?"

Surin followed his friend's gaze offshore. "We can *build* a pitch!"

Uncle Hemmin belly-laughed. "That's too difficult."

This didn't stop them from trying.

T he boys hauled wood scraps till their backs ached.

They collected nails till their fingers hurt.

They tied old barrels together till their hands chafed.

Day after day, they sawed.
Week after week, they hammered.
Laughter from the villagers shrouded them like dense fog.

The boys ignored it. They were building their dream.
Plank by plank.

Finally, their floating pitch was ready.
"Let's play!" yelled Surin.

There were
a few problems.

But nothing would stop them.

The swaying pitch taught the boys
to have better body balance.

The lack of a fence taught them
to have better ball control.

The slippery surfaces taught them
to have better footing.

Day after day, more and more villagers stood on the rickety-crickety walkways to watch the boys practice.

"Good pass! Great kick!"
the villagers cheered.

Even Uncle Hemmin watched from outside his café. "They are tough and strong-willed. Qualities that make champions," he admitted.

They all agreed the boys made a promising team.

One day, the boys journeyed on longtail boats to the mainland.

They played team after team in the district tournament.

"You boys are ridiculous! Ridiculously good football players!" shouted Uncle Hemmin.

Lek stole the ball and chipped it down the field. Krit dribbled and spun around defenders. Surin aimed and fired—

SCORE!

"Great game," said a player from the opposing team.
"Your team has got some sharp skills."

The boys hadn't won the tournament.
"But you worked hard and never gave up," said
Uncle Hemmin. "You are champions anyway."

Every evening, villagers young and old still gathered to watch the boys play.

"I'm going to be like them someday," said Lek's little sister. "A football player!"

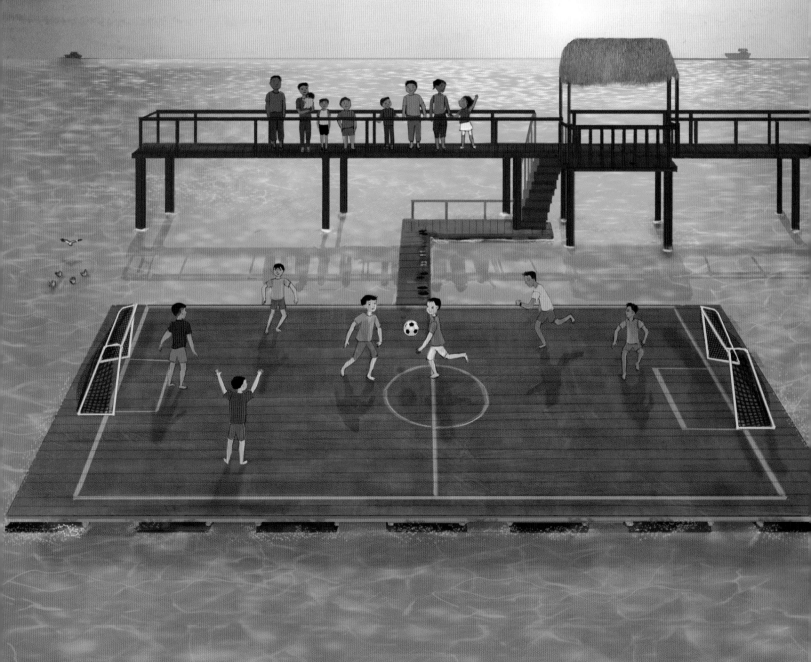

In the billowy bay waters, hidden in the shadows of towering limestone cliffs, atop a network of stilts, floats the village of Koh Panyee.

In that village, a group of boys built their own place to play. They formed the town's first official youth football league. They made the game a pillar of their community and inspired future generations of kids.

All because they had followed their dream.

# AUTHOR'S NOTE

Back in 2013, I saw a humanitarian commercial about a group of boys who loved football but had no place to play. I watched that video over and over. I was inspired by how the boys faced their environmental and societal challenges with perseverance, hope, and ingenuity. I wanted kids everywhere to know about them.

I based this fictional story on real events that happened in the village of Koh Panyee in southern Thailand. Koh Panyee is an arrangement of homes and walkways built on top of stilts to keep them above the high tide waters. A determined group of boys loved to watch football (called *soccer* in the United States and Canada), but with no usable land, they didn't have a pitch, an outdoor playing field for sports. In 1986, the boys constructed a floating pitch made from scrap material that could withstand the tides. The floating pitch presented unique challenges. The boys had to stay distributed around the pitch, so it didn't tip up! The pitch also forced them to practice better ball control. A ball in water was a foul, which meant someone was going for a swim. The boys lost a lot of games in the beginning, but eventually, they started winning competitions on the mainland.

Today the island has one permanent pitch built on stilts and one floating pitch. The boys eventually formed the first official youth football team of Koh Panyee and became one of the best youth leagues in southern Thailand. They created a tradition that is still alive today.

Writing children's books is my dream. I hope young readers will be inspired to pursue their interests and realize it is up to them to make their dreams come true.

# ILLUSTRATOR'S NOTE

I am honored to bring my art to this story. I was born in Krung Thep (Bangkok), Thailand, and it is part of my goal as a children's book illustrator to help bring more diversity to books available to children. Drawing Thai characters is one of my favorite ways to do so. It feels as familiar as drawing pictures of my own family.

Though I grew up in the United States, we traveled back on several occasions and have visited Thailand's southern regions. I recalled the emerald waters and lush island scenery as I created the art. I drew typical wooden houses, shops, and colorfully painted buildings. People-watching in Thailand informed my choice of clothing for the characters. Most dress casually in modern T-shirts with jeans or shorts, while others wear more traditional garb, such as woven sarong skirts.

While the boys in this story are from Thailand, people from all over the world can relate to their love of football, their persistence, and ultimately their celebration of success after their accomplishments.